By Laura Williams
Translated by Emma Svensson

© 2022 Williams Books
1 rue de l'église, 91430 Igny
Dépôt légal : Décembre 2022
ISBN 978-2-494614-51-2
Imprimé à la demande par Amazon
Loi n° 49-956 du 16 juillet 1949 sur les publications destinées à la jeunesse

äpple

apple

avokado

avocado

banan

banana

bönor

beans

kål

cabbage

morot

carrot

chili

chilli

majs

corn

gurka

cucumber

aubergine

eggplant

vitlök

garlic

ingefära

ginger

gröna bönor

green beans

guava

guava

citron

lemon

mango

mango

svamp

mushroom

lök

onion

orange

orange

papaya

papaya

passionsfrukt

passion fruit

jordnöt

peanut

ärtor

peas

ananas

pineapple

potatis

potato

pumpa

pumpkin

ris

rice

soja

soy

spenat

spinach

sockerrör

sugar cane

sötpotatis

sweet potato

tomat

tomato

vattenmelon

watermelon

vete

wheat

Thank you

Thank you for purchasing "Swedish-English Words for Toddlers"! Your support means a lot to me, and I hope you and your child enjoy these books.

If you have a moment, I would greatly appreciate it if you could leave a review on Amazon. Your feedback will help me improve future editions of the series and create more resources for bilingual children.

Thank you again for your support. You can access the reviews on Amazon by scanning the QR code below or by visiting the link below:

https://www.amazon.com/review/create-review?&asin=2494614511

Thank you for helping me continue my work as a language teacher and translator. Your support is greatly appreciated!

In the same collection

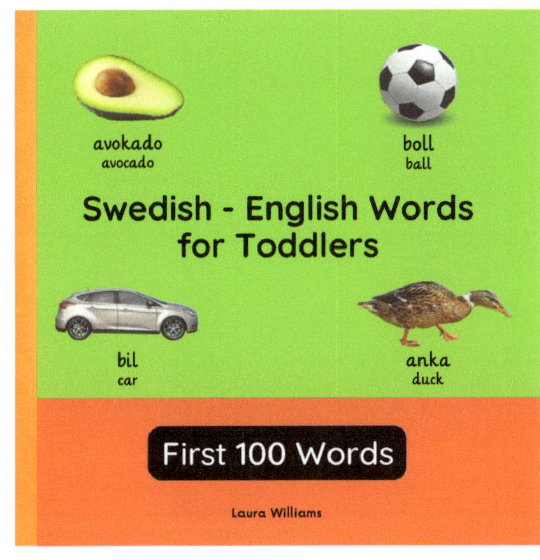

www.ingramcontent.com/pod-product-compliance
Lightning Source LLC
LaVergne TN
LVHW071655180726
843512LV00002B/454